# WALSALL AS IT WAS

by

John Benson and Trevor Raybould

**Front Cover:** From Saint Paul's Street (on the site of the present Bus Centre) looking towards Darwall Street. On the right are old houses and the Blue Coat School. The Blue Coat School was erected in 1858-9 at a cost of about £5,600. On the left, Saint Paul's Close and, in the distance, Saint Matthews. Date c. 1912 or a little earlier.

First edition September 1978
Second impression September 1988

Published by Hendon Publishing Co., Ltd., Hendon Mill, Nelson, Lancs.

Text © John Benson and Trevor Raybould, 1978.

Printed by Turner & Earnshaw Ltd., Westway House, Sycamore Avenue, Burnley, Lancs.

**Introduction and Acknowledgements:** In this book we have tried to provide readers with a selection of photographs of Walsall and the surrounding districts in the late nineteenth and early twentieth centuries. Unfortunately shortage of space and unavailability of photographs preclude a complete coverage although we believe that these photographs, few of which have ever been published before, do show many aspects of life in Victorian and Edwardian Walsall. We hope therefore that the book will be of interest to all those concerned with the history of this part of South Staffordshire.

We are very grateful for the help which we have received in the preparation of this book. We particularly wish to thank Mr. F. H. Lamb, Director of the Walsall Metropolitan Borough Library and Museum Services, for his interest and encouragement. Without his help the book would probably never have been completed. We are also grateful to Mr. P. F. Farmer; Mr. A. J. R. Hickling; Mr. A. J. Mealey, Reference Librarian at Walsall Central Library; Mr. H. J. H. Nelson of the Hendon Publishing Company; the *Birmingham Evening Mail* and the *Walsall Observer* which published our appeal for photographs; and to Mr. J. Fraser, of West Bromwich College of Technology, and Mr. Graham Farrell, of The Polytechnic, Wolverhampton, both of whom reproduced photographs for us.

Our thanks are due to the following individuals and institutions for allowing us to reproduce the photographs included in the book (the figures refer to plate numbers); Mr. A. J. R. Hickling, 36-38; Walsall Central Library, Local History Collection, Front Cover, 1, 7-14, 16-35, 39-44, 46-48, 50-51, 53, 59-68, Back Cover; Walsall Central Library, Meikle Collection, 2-6, 15, 45, 49, 52, 54-58, 69.

John Benson<br>
Trevor Raybould.

**1.** The Bridge, Walsall about the end of the nineteenth century, looking towards Digbeth with Saint Matthews Church in the distance. Sister Dora's statue is clearly visible on the left of the picture. The monument was erected in 1886 in grateful memory of Sister Dora (see plate 63). Note that only certain areas of the street were cobbled: along the tramlines and for the convenience of pedestrians crossing to the market in Digbeth. Covered waggons, typical of the period, may be seen approaching from the direction of the High Street.

**2.** The Dining Room of the "George" Hotel. The "George" Hotel was built by Mr. Thomas Fletcher in 1781 to serve as a coaching inn at the time of various road improvements which placed Walsall on the main route from Birmingham to Stafford. In 1823 the front of the building was altered by the addition of the handsome portico and Ionic columns which were brought from Fisherwick Hall.

**3–5.** Left and top right. The rear of the "George" Hotel, (pulled down c.1934). Three pictures of a town centre yard towards the end of the last century. They provide a striking illustration of the close intermingling of home and leisure within a very restricted area.

**6.** Bottom. The view from Digbeth up the High Street at the beginning of the present century. In the distance may be seen the Green Dragon and the Guildhall (see plate 7).

**7.** The Dragon (formerly the Green Dragon) Hotel in High Street — held by Thomas Fletcher before constructing The George in 1781. It was rebuilt in the 1770s at the time of improvements to the adjoining Guildhall. At different periods the assembly room at the hotel was used by Methodists, Catholics and Baptists. To the right stands the Italianate facade of the Guildhall, redesigned in 1865-7, to include a council chamber and corporation offices. The date of the photograph is firmly established by the early phonographs in the shop to the left.

**8.** Upper Bridge Street on the site of the Central Co-op. Note the bollards and the handsome gas lamp. Gas was first provided in Walsall by the gas works built by the Improvement Commissioners in 1826 (on a site later covered by Arboretum Road). It proved inadequate to meet the needs of the growing population, and the Commissioners constructed a new works in Wolverhampton Street in 1850. In 1876 the Corporation took over the interests of the Commissioners and in the following year opened the large gas works at Pleck.

**9.** Upper Rushall Street looking towards High Street at the end of the 1890s with Saint Matthews off to the left. The "Roe Buck" inn was one of many in the vicinity of the market area along Digbeth and High Street. Even more prominent is the large, ornate pawnbroker's sign (Preston) gracing the fine eighteenth century building on the near left corner.

**10.** A photograph of Town End Bank taken in 1885, showing the town weighing machine. This was a notoriously poor and squalid area which was cleared under the compulsory powers of purchase granted by the Artisans Dwelling Act of 1875. A pawnbroker's shop and two inns can also be seen in the picture.

**11.** Top left. The junction of Holtshill Lane with Lower Rushall Street looking towards the Arboretum. On the left is the entrance to Intown Row starting its winding route down to Lichfield Street. Limestone was once a common feature of buildings in this area as can be seen from the house on the left. Beyond the inn with its popular "Pure Home Brewed Ales" sign the older properties dating from the early seventeenth century can be picked out by their distinctive gable roofs.

**12.** Bottom left. The old workhouse in Victoria Road, Darlaston. A contrast to the "purpose built" union workhouses of the nineteenth century (see the following picture). Dating from about 1700, the old workhouse was demolished in 1887 to make way for the Town Hall.

**13.** Right. A view of the Walsall Union Workhouse (now the Manor Hospital), taken in January, 1912. It was erected in 1838 at a cost of £7,600 and was enlarged to meet the growing needs of the local population during the nineteenth century. In addition to the town area, the Union included Aldridge, Bloxwich, Great Barr, Bentley, Darlaston, Pelsall, Rushall and Walsall Wood.

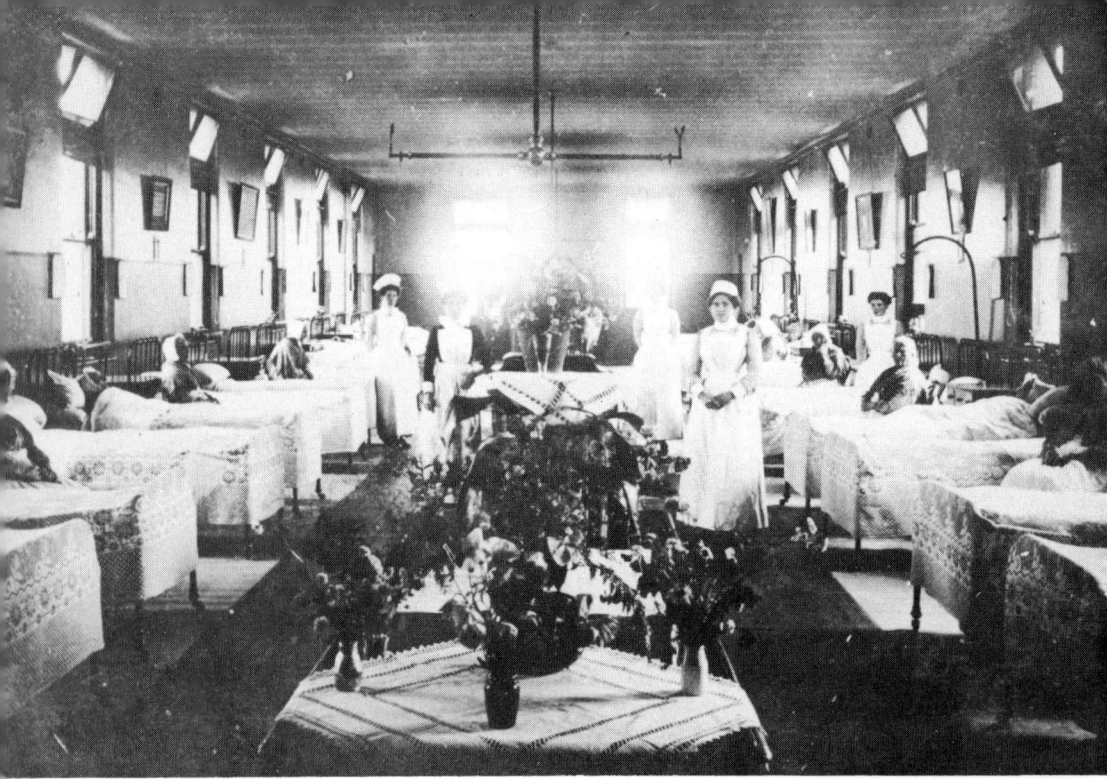

**14–16.** Left and top right. The inside of the workhouse in 1910, a couple of years before the previous picture was taken. The first photograph shows the Infirmary which had been opened in 1896 and which, with its flowers and bed covers, is far removed from the "typical" workhouse scene. The other two pictures, of the kitchen and the laundry, show the other side of institutional living, with the large number of staff needed to cater for the requirements of the inmates.

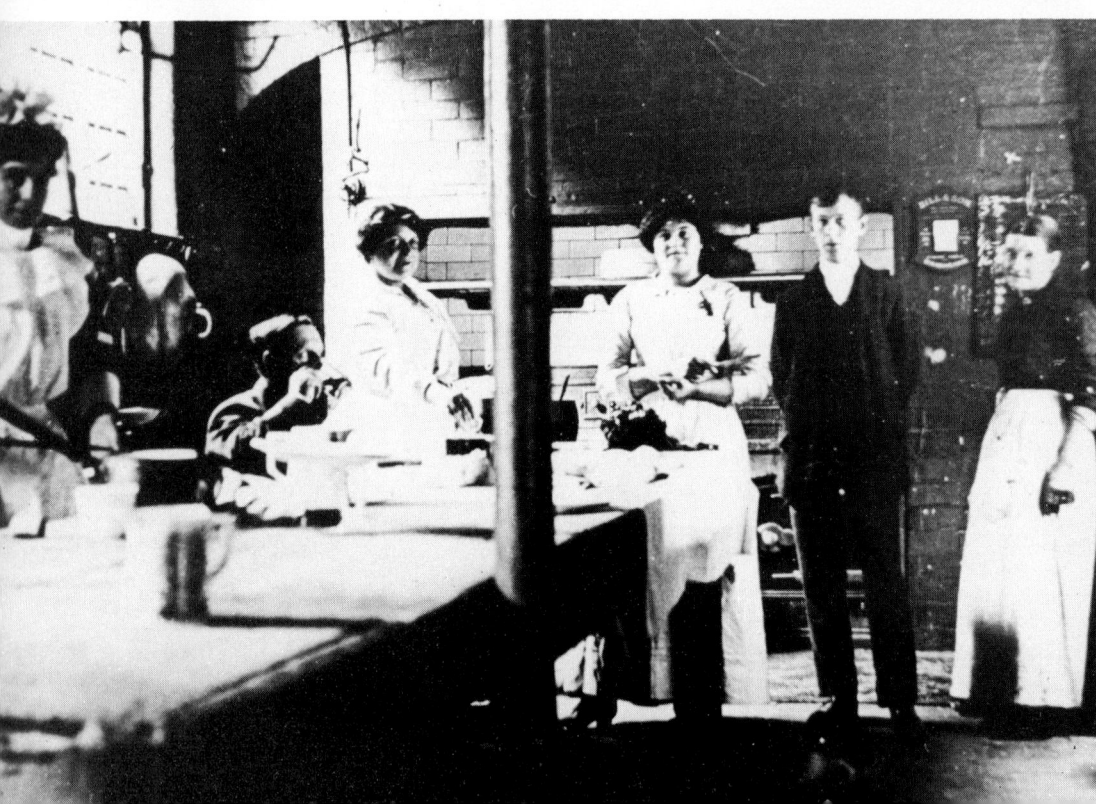

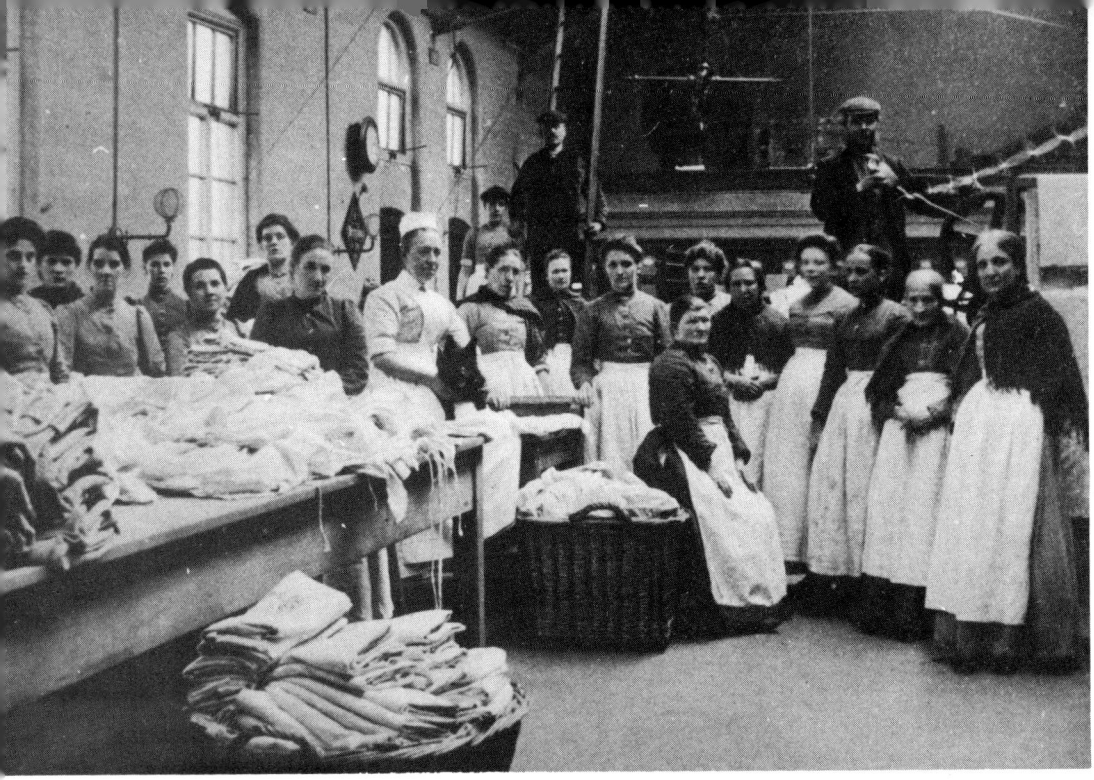

**17.** Bottom. The Free Library from the College of Arts, in Goodall Street. With the growing concern for literacy and self-improvement, provision of libraries was a major interest of socially aware Victorians. The Free Library, built in the classical style, was established in 1859 and was supported by a 1d. rate and voluntary subscriptions.

**18.** Left. The Municipal Baths, opened in 1896, before the building of the Town Hall. The building on the left is probably the Liberal Club. The photograph was taken from the site of the present Library.

**19.** Right. The Town Hall entrance under construction — a useful focal point for advertisements in the days of cheap travel when a day trip to Worcester on the Midland Railway cost 2/9. Walsall's new Council House and Town Hall was erected at a cost of £101,000 and opened in 1905. (See plates 66–67).

**20.** After a second major visitation of cholera in 1849, Walsall, along with other local towns, sought ways of improving the quality of the water supply. The South Staffordshire Waterworks Co. was formed in 1853 and John Robinson McClean who had built London's drainage system was engaged as engineer. Water was pumped from the New Red Sandstone rocks to the reservoir at Brownhills whence it fed the Pleck reservoir by gravity. In this photograph of the new pumping station off Lichfield Road, taken in 1857, the scale of the operation is apparent from the massive buttresses employed to enable the building to withstand the vibration generated by the enormous steam pumps.

**21.** Typical of many of the older streets of Walsall is this street (possibly Tantarra Street) with the bow window, high-stepped entrance and doorway suggesting an early nineteenth century origin. A narrow entry between this and the adjoining shop gives access to the rear of the premises. Further up the hill a handsome town house complete with portico and ornamented railings stands next to a building which may be a small workshop. Most of the buildings have a coal cellar. The pavement of Staffordshire blue bricks, stone curbs and cobbled gutter complete the scene.

**22.** A nineteenth-century shop grafted onto a terrace of large houses dating from the early and mid-eighteenth century. The rear of this terrace has a wide cobbled entrance for carriages and carts. A brewhouse, so characteristic of the region, stands behind the shop. It may have a central chimney and, if this is the case, it could also have been used as a small forge with a central hearth. The prominent advertisement for "home brewed ales" suggests that the crude one-storey building is a beer shop. It is surprising to find an advertisement for pianos and organs at a Birmingham address. Perhaps this location stands on the main tram route to Birmingham.

**23.** Large eighteenth and early nineteenth century houses were frequently converted to other uses during the latter years of the last century as can be seen from this once elegant house. Street improvements as yet extended only to pavements and drainage; horse manure, that curse of pedestrians, litters the street.

**24.** The start of a new working day for man and beast. Residential accommodation interspersed with shops and small workshop premises line this wide but poorly surfaced street. Advertisements abound in the age before television. This type of cart was once familiar throughout the Black Country particularly for the transport of coal. The church at the top of the hill is probably St. Andrew's at Birchills.

**25.** The top of Church Hill at the corner of Temple Street looking towards Hill Street. This narrow, winding and unpaved street is typical of the older residential areas near the town centre. Some attempt was made to improve the roadway by the use of granite cobbles in the gutters to reduce wear from the passage of iron-rimmed cart wheels and to improve drainage. Stone curbs helped to protect the raised pavement surfaced with hard-wearing Staffordshire "blues" which are easily distinguished by their diamented pattern.

**26.** At the corner of this wide thoroughfare (New Street) stands the Blue Pig Inn. From the external appearance it was probably built in the seventeenth century. The tall three storey house adjoining it illustrates the change in scale which had taken place by the eighteenth century. Opposite stands a cheap lodging house used by "WORKING MEN TRAVELLERS". This photograph was taken in a dry period: the rough unsurfaced road would become a quagmire in the winter.

**27.** A quiet residential road near the town centre showing a line of Victorian villas. These provide an indication of the air of respectable privacy with which middle class professional and business men liked to surround themselves. The street is significantly clean. (Compare plate 23).

**28.** The Parish Church of Saint Michael, Rushall was originally a chapel-of-ease to Walsall. It was rebuilt in 1858 and it is possible that the photograph was taken at the time of improvements to the tower in 1867.

**29.** John Wesley's Meeting House in Bilston Street, Wednesbury (?). Note the use of cast iron curbs because iron was so plentiful and cheap in the Black Country.

**30.** A view of King Street, Darlaston, c.1888. In contrast to our own day, the streets are clear and the pavements are cluttered with advertisements and wares.

**31.** Tramway relaying at Wednesbury Road, The Pleck c.1910. This was part of the programme of improvements after the Town Council decided to municipalise the tramways in March, 1903.

**32–33.** Progress in public transport: compare the photographs of the two trams taken at an interval of about ten years. The high-funnelled steam tram at Wednesbury, the upper "deck" open to the elements, stirs the imagination more than the trimmer new electric tram climbing the incline at Walsall Wood in 1910. These more modern trams were introduced in the early twentieth century.

**34–35.** Despite the growing popularity of the railways, accidents continued to occur. These photographs show just two, one from the middle of the century and one from the end. The first was taken in 1859 at Elwell's Pool, Bescot on the South Staffordshire line. The second dates from October 1899 when a goods train ran into the London express at Portobello in the morning fog.

36–38. Walsall has long had close ties with the coal mining industry. These three pictures show just a few of the 250 or so men and boys employed at the Walsall Wood colliery at the beginning of this century. The photographs give a good impression both of the hard physical effort needed to cut the coal and of the great difficulty experienced in keeping the underground roadways safe and secure.

**39.** The demolition of the "Khyber Pass" towards the end of the last century. The precise nature and location of the "Pass" is not known although it may have been part of an old colliery railway and was probably situated in the Rough Hay area for in the distance may be seen the well known Dudley-Sedgley ridge.

**40.** The Town Council was by far the most important institution in late nineteenth century Walsall, with its standing committees being responsible for such local services as gas, sewage and lighting, cemeteries, baths and parks and the library and art gallery. We see here a meeting of the thirty-four strong Council in 1897 under the chairmanship of the Mayor, Councillor William Smith. The Council met in the Guildhall on the High Street (see plate 7), an impressive building which had been erected in 1734 and rebuilt in 1863.

**41.** The three councillors for Darlaston pose proudly in about 1904. They are Charles Foster, John Whitehouse, Jr., and George Wiley.

**42.** The members of Darlaston Fire Brigade in about 1900. By this date most towns had established their own fire services. At Walsall for example the Brigade consisted of a captain and thirteen firemen, who had the use of a manual engine, two telescopic fire escapes and two steam engines, one of which was capable of delivering 300 gallons, and the other 450 gallons, a minute.

**43.** An 1896 meeting of the Walsall School Board at the Board's offices in Bradford Street, shortly before its functions were taken over by the Education Committee of the Town Council in 1902. In 1896 the members of the Board were responsible for the running of ten schools and among those present at this meeting may be identified the Rev. W. S. Swayne, who later became Bishop of Lincoln, and, in the foreground, the vice-chairman of the Board, Miss Brace.

**44.** In the early years of the century, as today, it was not always easy to ensure regular attendance at school. We see here one of the methods which was adopted: a group of the best attenders at Brownhills Central School pose, for the camera in 1910. William Coates is second from the right on the back row.

**45.** An unusual view of one of Walsall's two courts, the Borough Magistrates' Court, in session in the Guildhall. At the end of the last century the work of the court was carried out by thirty-one magistrates, a recorder, a coroner and a clerk of the peace.

**46–48.** Left and top right. Walsall, like every other town and city, had a large number of public houses. Drinking offered an escape — however brief — from the harsh realities of life and was undoubtedly the most popular recreation among the Victorian and Edwardian working class. These photographs show three popular local public houses.

Top left. This picture of the "White Hart" inn at Caldmore Green was probably taken shortly after the improvements of 1884. The inn was built in the late seventeenth century by George Hawe and was originally the home of the Hawe family.

Bottom left. A less attractive, though more typical, drinking place, the "Brown Jug Inn", at Sand Beds, Lanehead in Willenhall. The exact date of this photograph is not known although it was almost certainly taken around the turn of the century.

Top right. It is unusual to discover interior photographs of Victorian and Edwardian public houses so this picture of the "Blue Pig" on New Street is of particular interest. The English and foreign graffiti, below which the customers pose, are almost impossible to understand at this distance in time.

**49.** Bottom left. For those of a more active disposition Walsall could offer a wide range of sporting activities. At the end of the last century there were clubs and societies catering, amongst other things, for football, cricket, gymnastics, swimming, athletics, cycling, chess, and bowling In this picture we see the members of one of the more unusual of these organisations, the Walsall Quoiting Club.

**50.** Football was of course very popular. This picture shows the Rushall Rovers team in 1878 at the very time that interest was really growing in what was to become our national sport. The Rovers' playing strip, with its scarves, caps, plus fours and heavy boots, is of particular interest to us today.

**51.** A well known local character, James "Grab" Soliness, the trainer of the Walsall Swifts Football Club. The "Swifts" amalgamated with second division Walsall Town Football Club in about 1898, the year in which Walsall won the Birmingham Cup for the second year in succession by beating Wolverhampton Wanderers by three goals to nil.

**52.** The start of a walking match from Walsall town centre at the beginning of this century, at the height of what was known as "the walking fever".

**53.** Motor cycling was also becoming popular at around the turn of the century and this picture shows a rally which was held at Willenhall in 1911. By the eve of the First World War there were seven motor cycle dealers in Walsall, with Hough & Co. having two branches, one in Wolverhampton Street and one on the Bloxwich Road.

**54.** Some local men joined the Volunteers. In 1897 for instance the Second Volunteer Battalion of the South Staffordshire Regiment had seventeen officers, twenty-one sergeants, twenty corporals, five buglers and three hundred and thirty-eight privates, a total of four hundred and one men. This picture shows members of the Battalion moving from the yard at the back of the 'George' (see plates 3 — 5).

**55.** The Volunteers, plus camp followers, on a visit to Fairbourne, across the River from Barmouth, on the Welsh coast. It has not been possible to date this picture exactly but it was taken some time during the 1880s, at a time when the Battalion's strength stood at about 250.

**56.** Nothing is known either about the people enjoying themselves on this outing but like the previous picture it was one of those taken by William Meikle around the turn of the century. Meikle was Walsall's leading photographer at this time. In 1895, for example, the visitors to Walsall Amateur Photographic Society's exhibition voted him the winner of the silver medal for the best picture on show.

57–58. That well known local photographer, William Meikle, not only took these pictures of his friends at Sutton; he also organised the trip (which had started from the George Hotel in the centre of Walsall) and took many other excellent photographs of Walsall and the surrounding district, some of which are reproduced in this book.

**59.** Walsall's first theatre was opened here in The Square in 1803 and was often visited by Charles Kean, Foote and other famous actors. By the time this photograph was taken at the end of the century, the theatre had been turned into "The Crown" public house.

**60.** A view of the Imperial Theatre (formerly the St. George's Theatre) on Darwell Street around the turn of the century. Run by the Walsall Theatre Company, it had a capacity of 2,000, of whom 1,600 could be seated.

**61.** Two other Walsall theatres in the early years of the present century. In the foreground, on Park Street, is the Grand Theatre which, like the Imperial, was run by the Walsall Theatre Trust. In the background is Her Majesty's Theatre which had been opened by the Mayor on March 24th, 1900. It was built on the site of the old Town End Bank by Messrs. Whittaker & Co. of Dudley; its stage was sixty feet wide, forty-five feet deep and fifty-five feet high and it had a seating capacity of 2,000.

**62.** Left. The employees of the London and North Western Railway presenting a pony and carriage to Walsall's most famous personality, Sister Dora, in 1871 in recognition of "her tender deeds and patient nursings to many of themselves". Sister Dora (nee Dorothy Wyndlow Pattison) was born in Yorkshire in 1832, joined the Sisterhood of Good Samaritans in 1864 and first came to Walsall in the following year to help at the recently opened Cottage Hospital. It was from the hospital, and all through the smallpox epidemics of 1868-9, that she devoted herself to "thirteen years nursing and watching ministry among the suffering of the district" until her death on Christmas Eve 1878.

**63.** Right. Soon after Sister Dora's death a memorial window was placed in the parish church and a fund raised for sending patients to convalescent homes. Then on October 11th, 1886, a statue of Sister Dora was unveiled in the town centre. The occasion was marked, according to contemporary reports, "by a display of enthusiasm seldom before equalled in the town". The procession travelled from the Hospital to The Bridge where a crowd estimated at about 30,000 assembled to watch the ceremony. In the evening a banquet was held at St. George's Hall, the poor were feasted and a display of fireworks was organised in Bradford Place.

**64.** Left. Royal occasions always brought out the crowds. Queen Victoria's Jubilee in 1887, for example, was greeted with great enthusiasm all over the country. In this picture we see celebrations at the Bull Stake, Darlaston and it is interesting to notice the steam tram and, even in good weather, the appalling state of the road.

**65.** Right. The laying of the foundation stone of the Science and Art Institute in Bradford Place on June 20th, 1887. At this date classes were being held on Music, Art, Education, Magnetism and Electricity, Chemistry, Building and Machine Construction and Drawing, Hygene, Human Physiology, Sound Light and Heat, Geology, Physiography, Metallurgy, Iron and Steel, Chemical Analysis, Laboratory Practice, Mathematics, Natural Philosophy, Botany, Political Economy, Inorganic Chemistry, Principles of Mining, French, German, Latin, English Grammar, Arithmetic, Shorthand and Reporting.

**66–67.** Prince Christian of Shleswig-Holstein laid the foundation stone of the new Town Hall on May 29th, 1902. As this was the first visit of royalty to the town since the time of Charles I, it was an occasion of great celebration and enjoyment. The scale of the lunch held in Prince Christian's honour at the Corporation Baths testifies to the importance with which the event was viewed. The Town Hall was formally opened by the Mayor, Alderman (later Sir) E. T. Holden three years later on September 27th, 1905.

**68.** A bonfire to put our modern Guy Fawkes celebrations to shame. This enormous bonfire — it must be all of twenty feet high — was built by Darlaston District Council in honour of the coronation of King George V on June 22nd, 1911.

**69.** The coming of the circus was always a popular occasion. This photograph was taken from outside the George Hotel at around the turn of the century. The precise date is not known although the large numbers of flags which are visible suggest that it must have been a time of some national or local celebration.

**The Authors:** John Benson was born at Reading in 1945 and educated at the Royal Liberty Grammar School, Romford, Essex, and the Universities of Leicester, Leeds and Manitoba. He has taught at Sunderland Polytechnic, Lady Mabel College of Education and The Polytechnic, Wolverhampton, where he is now Senior Lecturer in History. His publications include *Rotherham As It Was*, with Robert G. Neville, (Hendon Publishing Co. Ltd., 1976).

Trevor Raybould was born in Tipton in 1935 and educated at Dudley Grammar School and the University of Bristol, followed by research at the Universities of Kent and Birmingham. He has taught at the West Midlands College of Education and is now Principal Lecturer in History at The Polytechnic, Wolverhampton, where he is also Director of the Centre for West Midland Historical Studies.